ENCOUNTERS FOR THE LIVING AND THE DEAD

Praise for ENCOUNTERS FOR THE LIVING AND THE DEAD

"Become mollusk. Notice when these poems crack you open. Notice when you are reading from your soft places. Your calcified shells. Notice the intimate irritant becoming pearl. Mollusks chemosynthesize the radioactive isotopes of volatile earth in the broken places at the bottom of the ocean. This too is the work of these poems. Become mollusk and notice what changes."

—ALEXIS PAULINE GUMBS, author of
Survival is a Promise: The Eternal Life of Audre Lorde

"*Encounters for the Living and the Dead* is a beguiling complexity of creative sensibility. This collection of poetry offers a multiplicity of poetic responses to the questions of time, memory, being, and un-being.

"Jameela Dallis writes inside the sharp, blunt, but tender internal blade of holy allegiances to wishbones with hopes and allows her pen to decipher and translate the shards of vessels that held prayers. Her inaugural publication is a gaze turned inward with the concerns of conquest, immersion, surrender, and power portrayed with dynamic textures, ekphrasis, and sublime boundaries of craft that capture and demonstrate her sensuous parlous relationship with the sea."

—JAKI SHELTON GREEN, North Carolina Poet Laureate

"Jameela F. Dallis is a poet of the senses, lush and unambiguous. Everything—desire and the body's tidal response to its lunar pull, a meal's layers of mineral and green and sea tang, and even grief's 'silked mimosa flowers / abscised and suddenly absent'—appeals to the body and, thus, honors it, and, by honoring it, honors the poet's ancestors, honors 'alltheshes.' This is a book of assertions, of naming the self and, by naming, transforming the self into what she wants to be in any moment—witness, oyster, something craved, stretched canvas, perfumed rice, morning glory—in all the vibrancy of true attention, to become a capital-E Experience beyond the limits of ordinary (read: colonial, capitalist) imagination into the altarworks of Dallis, an oracle of her own rush and rest, 'Who channels, who listens, who speaks, who dances' in these poems unlike anything I have ever read."

—EMILIA PHILLIPS, author of *Nonbinary Bird of Paradise*

"This book, in all its lushness, bravery, and vulnerability reminds me that a feast is not just about abundance, it is also a ceremony, a marking of the sacred. Jameela F. Dallis's *Encounters for the Living and the Dead* invites me into that ceremony so I might interrogate my own relationship to grief and ongoingness. 'I ate that oyster. / Inhaled decay as it flittered in / my mouth . . .' So few of us are willing to experience life fully if it means being confronted with our deepest hungers and the deep harms we have been forced to live through. So few of us can sit with the living and the dead with the kind of generosity that Dallis does, the deep curiosity, the love. This book stays with me. It fills me with wonder and hope."

—GABRIELLE CALVOCORESSI, author of *The New Economy*

JAMEELA F. DALLIS

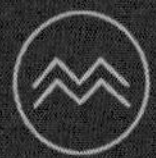

RIVER RIVER BOOKS
Durham, North Carolina

ENCOUNTERS FOR THE LIVING AND THE DEAD

Published in the United States of America

Library of Congress Cataloging-in-Publication Data
Dallis, Jameela F., 1985
Encounters for the Living and the Dead / Jameela F. Dallis.
ISBN-13: 979-8-9881378-8-7
Subjects: LCSH: American Poetry, Southern Literature, Visual Art.
LCGFT: Poetry.
Library of Congress Control Number: 2025933386

Cover art: Cornelis de Heem, *Still-Life with Oysters, Lemons and Grapes*, c. 1660s
Cover and interior design by Alban Fischer

RIVER RIVER BOOKS
10 Linganore Place
Durham, NC 27707

www.RiverRiverBooks.org

for my past and future selves

CONTENTS

3: EKPHRASTIC ENCOUNTERS

CODA

My heart is like an oyster shell, the Beloved's phantom is the pearl; now I am no more contained, for this house is filled with Him.

— JALĀL AD-DĪN MUHAMMAD RŪMĪ
Mystical Poems of Rūmī, trans. by A. J. Arberry

Falling in love, the otherness of the other, is the greatest joy; and vulnerability in the face of the other is a sweet surrender, a gift rather than a sacrifice. The other's potential to make me better than I am is the power of love. . . . To love is to bear witness to the process of witnessing that gives us the power to be, together. And being together is the chaotic adventure of subjectivity.

— KELLY OLIVER
Witnessing: Beyond Recognition

No matter what has happened in our past, when we open our hearts to love we can live as if born again, not forgetting the past but seeing it in a new way, letting it live inside us in a new way.

— bell hooks
All About Love: New Visions

BLACK, HOLY TIME

A portal is a conduit to transformation and a star's death is varnished with black, holy time. Ecstatic pedestrians move between spaces with grace and some whispered conjure or cross-signed blessing on their foreheads.

I am witness. Portal is lined with humming: echoes from dreams and red earth and rustles of petticoats, cotton voile, and touches in the night.

Secret histories channeled and the wounded unstitch themselves so we can see their bones chalkwhite against skin glistening beneath asteroid belt, Polaris, and heat. Unstitched, unraveled, undone they become loud enough to enter dreams—oneiric pedestrians who just want to kiss the lunula of their beloveds.

I am witness. Portal is lined with voices: tongues from Babel, Georgia, Mississippi, Carolina, Tennessee, and mountain laurel growing toward light in Appalachian hills and hollers.

Who channels, who listens, who speaks, who dances? Who unstitches untruths and threads the needle with caterpillar silk? Who channels, who listens, who speaks, who dances? Who unweaves the rice, coffee, and gold dust that hold prayers, blood, and vision? What pedestrians gave up sole and hip and hamstring to waltz under cover of new moon?

I am witness. Portal is lined with shuffles: feet that run and creep and dangle. Feet that long to return to the Atlantic where pedestrians sink toes into sand and emerge newly pavé.

But who can return? How is return woven into flesh, cries, or wishes placed on altars? Return is sewn into cotton housedresses, leather boots left on the porch, and handkerchiefs. Return erupts from hymns and hums and guitar strings. It's found in woolly curls and broad noses and proud foreheads. Return lives in pedestrians ecstatic to walk without fear.

And I am witness. Hewn and stitched with love and prayers. I do not fear the portal that conducts, contracts, and transforms. I do not fear the thread that binds me to those who walk between realms and through histories. As I am witness to starlight from long-dead origins, I am witness to them.

1. ALTARWORKS

I'm not a widow,
but two lovers I have lost.
And they left me love.

ANCESTORS

for Mary Prince

not just the sting of the whip, the nothingcoloredblue of the ocean
or the spaces so dark and putrid and red   black   brown fleshsmelling
or thrusts of the men alltheshes were forced to bathe
            and the children alltheshes were forced to birth, bury, and see carted off
because mistress hates that bitch with olive skin and thick silky plaits

but the time before the ocean

are memories of past lives memories of
ancestors' lives—   are my offerings enough?
what do our ancestors want?

INJURY

for my grandmother, Louise

I am afraid of becoming injured
the doctor with steel
blue eyes the nurse with flat-
ironed ash hair
        may not see my worth

        my being human
and dark
and comely like
        Solomon's lover

or

        not comely
        at all

BLUE

for Cora Kammer

Blue like imagined rain or periwinkle
covers thought of you thick as amber resin oozing
down rigid bark in northern places.

Blue is something you must have felt.
Drawn out and brazen, breathed brass and pined piano
all minors flats tense unexpected

Why blue and melancholy—blue and impenetrable happiness?
Why not the blue of irises: wild irises boy irises or those of a girl?
Why the cold numb blue beckoning blood tears inscrutable pain?

Until you answer, I will dream of you
clothed in the blue of cornflowers and sea islands intoxicated by electric
ashen cobalt swirls of sacred incense burned for you.

VALENTINE'S DAY

for Chandra Taylor Smith

Ghost cousin who loved ghosts
and
        dreamed of worlds beyond
ghastly love—

Today you died years ago and
I keep
        your picture on
my altar because because

you know that magic is
currents
        in our blood and these
currents come back from underneath.

You dreamed of Eileen Fisher,
new loves,
        and freedom—
triumph over cancer, but I

drew Defeat and it meant
I'd be
        writing this today. Death and
Valentine love wondering

what you'd say to me being
in love

and not with my love on
the day you died
but years on now.

TWO WINGS

for Randall Kenan

I remember Stephen King
and feeling seen
in your office with
                    open door

I remember your laugh filling
space rooms hallways porches gardens galaxies
your smile with
                    clever teeth

You anointed me "Ms. Gothic"
wished me "Godspeed" and thanked me
when I was
                    giving thanks

We talked Gothic this and horror that
and haunting and my proclivity for
bright fashion
                    in grey spaces

I remember that afterparty
you snuck me in saying say
you're with me
                    oh, Randall, keep making mischief
now you have
                    two wings

THREE OF SWORDS

for Todd Neal

There is an absence in my chest.
It is the shape of something I want to be haunted by.

Someone I want to be here,
or there beside me,
or in the bed we never shared.

Be that shadow that stands at the corner of my sleep.
Be that spectre that wraps me in warm
the color of rose-worn pink or
the añejo we loved to nurse in the yard you never cared to tend.

I remember smelling the sweat, the turpentine—
that scent that was always always reminding me that you would die.
That scent the shape of something rotten, maybe fecund,
but still something I wish I could walk into again—

its memory is something that resurrects
my worry for you and then dissolves
into the absence, into that space that holds

the shape of what I'm reaching

toward. There is an absence in my chest.
It is the shape of someone I want to haunt me.

MIMOSAN

for Todd Neal

You, phantomed limb like
silked mimosa flowers
abscised and suddenly absent

(their fragrance a powdery haze like the
indelible smear of not-yet-dry ink).

You, lampblack on watercolor paper
swallow whole lobes of my being and
I wonder what it must be like to touch
the wound, the break—

and, then, does the tonic flow
in? Me, abandoned web pocked with dust
and clinging to the edge of a dream where

you are whole, rejoined
there like plumb, dancing
magenta blooms.

ONE SIDE OF THE BORDER

S------ walks in and doesn't let you say goodbye
everything is lilac
        heavy with scent that covers shit buried again and again at edge of self-field
until

one day s------ walks in and says it's time, and our lovers dream of us but
it's too late even if there's time—because s------ has been there moving along our
border-self
        waiting for ████████████████ rot to flood in.

S------ is lilac. Washed-out pride: a misplaced hue leaves them wondering fuming
bereft

        wishing you him her them me were still together on
one side of border

SEE ME NOW

"I ate the day / Deliberately, that its tang / Might quicken me all into verb, pure verb."
—MARY OLIVER, *"Oysters"*

The year I crossed the ocean four times, I only walked in once.
That felt wrong because I know the ocean is mother and her tides, white foam, and roaring breath return my call

because a part of me is always calling, remembering how it felt to wriggle in the sand—all mouth and hungry for more

all the time.

I remember crying on one of the most exquisite hotel rooftops in Marrakech surrounded by Black artists from all over the world—thinking about my ancestors who may have disembarked at Gadsden's Wharf: *if only* only *they could see me now.*

But I think they did. The nice ones and maybe the mean ones, too.

That's why I carry crystals in my change purse; heed crocodiles, alligators, and cassowaries in dreams. Defeat in the cards—I know better, now.

And since then and now, I have eaten and walked and flown and driven. All sweat and hope.

But that was the year everything got wet. Words ran down the pages of my journal. On my birthday. And I was falling in love with someone who didn't want me. Not the way I wanted him anyway.

if only they could see me now

Pomegranate seeds, rare ribeye, blistered shishito peppers. Rutabaga puree, benne seed furikake, cashew and miso brittle. Baked oysters and rock salt. Kaftans and wine I can't pronounce.

And later, I knew. And I cried and cried and—

savored some of the most beautiful meals of my life: Fine de Claires №3 from Oléron; Spanish sardines served with roasted lemon and smoked crème crue; a corn tostada with trout from Banka in Basque country, sorrel, and guindillas; toasted oat ice cream over a crumble and cherry liqueur

and I went back 2 days later.

if only they could see me now

strawberry foxglove, a chain of gold, tektite, citrine

Brittany, Rhode Island, Washington, North Carolina, Virginia, Massachusetts, New Jersey—I've eaten your oysters.

Grace Points, Bay River Selects, Tarheel Tiderunners from Stump Sound, Baywater Indigos, Topsail Jewels, Wellfleets, and Flying Points from Maine with a tasting note of roast chicken. Hammersleys that taste of cucumber with dark frilling, curling edges. Crisp, sweet Summerstones in shells bony as duck feet. Plump and meaty Calm Coves are good with a splash of lemon. Their shells recall barnacles. Unassuming and buttery, Kinnakeeters need a helping of mignonette.

The list is longer, but that's not what this is about.

This is about taking in the sea, remembering estuaries, imbibing ocean. And not drowning.

if only they could see me now

pearly everlasting, artemisia, nacre nacre nacre

And there's orange pinot gris from Alsace: notes of fresh green musky grape; it's cold and juicy; fabulous and beautiful.

A passerina from Abruzzo: melon, sweet but not cloyingly so. *Lovely*, I note.

And I could go on, but I won't. Because this is about drinking seawater, dreams that are estuaries, walking into the ocean. And the business of re-membering Toni Morrison was about.

This year I have entered ocean at least four times.

Returned to and left and returned again to my perch drenched in Yves Klein blue where I have dreamed and poemed. I bathed in the coral wet room, soaked and caught breath.

if only they could see me now

And in August the sun: a redorange fiery ball rising from mist; horizon obscured; teased cotton clouds. I watch sunrise at Carolina Beach and now I know the meaning of ruby-throated dawn.

And two months later in Durham, I see whisper of red above treeline. I'm standing in my sideyard in the dark—well past midnight—and aided by long exposure, I see aurora borealis, the wonderous Northern Lights

and with tears of wonder, I know, *I know*

they can see me now.

2: LES BÊTES DE LA MER

I am the love lobster.
I am satisfaction.
I clamor for you.

I, ORIGIN

after and for Lien Truong's I, Buffalo, *2017*

Himalayan black salt
and pink rare salmon swim into
the silver threads of
memory.

How long has this summer
black with death drug on
into lavender swaths of
audacious unconventional beauty?

RHYTHM, SURRENDER

after Robert Motherwell's Dance, *1981*

we dance unseen into midnight
joy thick as licorice
black, anise-ine

we become ancient
marine animals
blots beneath aeons of wet

our dance: squid ink surrender
lyric fluid undulating
like tendrils of jellyfish
piercing thin-skinned feet

LES BÊTES DE LA MER

after Henri Matisse's Les Bêtes de la Mer, *1950*

I have become one of
les bêtes de la mer.

In a silent way
though 200 years is at my
stoop knocking sounding
like rain
but my dreams know better
know how to speak through
oceans that birthed this rain.

I have become one of les bêtes de
la mer. Not a great white or a majestic orca.
Yet I am magic. Tender, fluid.

I am oyster. My ash black beard-like
frills on 5-year-old me's bobby socks.
Alabaster home, pearly mother.

I am become one of les bêtes de la mer
and I demand attention.
Look, look! I am a space of paradoxes
smooth and wild, protected yet free
I breathe in and out—filter 200 years
of yearning tied up in hungry
rain, parched from falling all night
chartreuse moss, charcoal crevices
spiny, molded shells—

I am become les bêtes de la mer
and my hot pink lips shoot fireworks
from flowerbeds, weave kelp into
my hair tying myself to another
home another space where others
have gone on and become beasts
of the deep.

Lapis blue, color I can't name
something with tendrils protecting
me you us from prying fingers.

MATERIAL ENCOUNTERS

after the exhibition of the same name
for Celia Gray, Harriet Hoover, Jean Gray Mohs, and the beings we love

IN THE BEGINNING, uneasy space fabric ticked and hummed.

Glossy threads hooked in and out.

Some quiet silken sheen washed the galaxy with tourmaline dust and iron ore and SOURCE pitched high and erupted hot mimosa nebulae scribbled and sculpted with lemon starburst and lobster red.

And stars brilliant as old cut diamonds, irregular and rare and white as crumbled Styrofoam on sunbaked asphalt filled the firmament.

WONDER sauntered in unexpectedly, felt vulnerable and curious, and with cottonsoft gesture and smile of discovery spoke into existence some new wild things wrapped in husks of beauty, breathborn sheaths of lilac, gray, silver, and clementine orange.

THEN, somewhere beyond a heath, hill, or a single mosshewn stone there came to be honeycombed reefs with pocked coral, abstract fish with dreamed-of rainbow fins, and angular branches of dancing evergreen seaweed where electric eels snake in and out of sapphire pools uncertain yet bold and alien with seemingly impossible ceramic scales and neon eyes spaceblack pupils in the depths of wet, bone-laden, and layered journeyways washed and awash.

Some loved-thing's carcass feeds a furstitched thing and lichen blooms in an Arctic tundra where iced earth and sea meet.

THE BEASTS OF THE SEA emerge encrusted with something akin to gold thread iridescent and regal, dazzling and beneath the beneath, volcanic issue bubbles up, deadly and indiscriminate.

Yet, THE BEASTS OF THE SEA dance as in light of daylight sun, both glinting and extravagant and humble and utilitarian because they know that love is a resilient thing somehow malleable as clay and as permanent as concrete because traces of it remain, telling a story of what has been cemented together whether misshapen or born from blueprint.

And these encounters with the materials of creation: velvet black, green sprout, ruby, feldspar pink, and phytoplankton blue are for the living and the dead, from SOURCE and WONDER and will persist as long as there is some thing as impossible and covetable as wing-spread or tucked-in-for-the-night love.

II

IN THE ___TH CHRONICLE OF LOVE, SOURCE whispered to WONDER and sweet osmanthus entered the breeze glossy, deeply green, linen white, and fragrant as orange blossom.

The envelope of DESIRE swelled. New lovers and old friends embraced. And everything was dazzling and dazzled. Those old-cut diamond stars streaked across sky like something from an early prophet's vision.

White-hot zircons that cooled and crystalized in newborn moon sparkle still after billions of years in corvid-black space. They themselves cousins or friends or parents of the eldest terrestrial minerals found in a greenveined, bruisedpurple gash of tanned leather earth some now call Jack Hills, Australia.

Sunflower sprouts reached toward cloudobscured sun—soft and hornworm green. Indigo shoots elegant and unbothered erupted and someone somewhere howled with abandon and the feeling of sunbeam.

Kingfishers left nests to hunt trout, minnow, and salmon in seven different storylines.

Hawks wrangled copper penny serpents and lightning-quick hares escaped into strawberry patches as red as the perfect lipstick.

DESIRE pulsed and writhed in satisfaction.

And SOURCE smiled.

NOW WONDER joins the place where ocean meets horizon and paints sky with blush, gold, ruby, and cerulean. Longabandoned shells wash onto shore and the paws of some fursoft being skip over sand with something near human joy but more expansive and untethered.

Japanese spider crab crawls ocean floor with algae crown and dreams of spiders Louise Bourgeois cast in bronze.

Brilliant beasts move through thresholds of wolfed nights and into diluvian expanse. Some are lured with snaps, and others wish for porcelain-white, wet bone spiraling nautilus.

Aquamarine seafish emerge from beryl green kelp forests waking from fantasies of vast coral: grassgreen and yellow as your French kitchen sponge.

So now you understand. THE BEASTS OF THE SEA dream, too.

And SOURCE pauses and waits for KISMET to rouse.

III

AND IN ANOTHER BEGINNING, KISMET stretched, squeezed eyes shut, opened mouth wide, and BEAUTY, SONG, and CHANCE emerged.

What melodies have played in the background of some softbodied humans falling in something akin to love? Fingers, hands, lips, eyes searching for another's something in twilight or spritz-fresh morning.

White-tipped ardor lingers in the wings—the edge of some ineffable thirdspace—waiting for another lover to leap, pirouette, or serenade gently into bliss.

What pleasure has some garnetcolored ranunculus or trumpet-shaped lilac bloom brought to some whiskered pup or cat, curious child, or cane-walking savant?

BEAUTY spread magenta, hydrangea mopheads, cranberry salvia, ornate orchids, and silvery lavender into hillsides, glens, jungles, hidden forests, and dales.

Something sweet and vermouthcolored began to flower and then somewhere deep and wet, a smack of jellyfish bloomed tendrils and beamed luminescent.

Still, there are more lovely things: Zambian emeralds, pink diamonds, skyblue zircons, and unshucked Fine de Claire oysters on ice in Grace Jones's dressing room.

CHANCE walks out of some impossible salt lake, naked and glistening, creating ripples in water pink as Sakura blossoms or cotton candy.

THEN, SONG shakes and transforms into opera.

NOW KISMET swims beyond horizon in ocean sublime and encounters pod of ancient humpbacks and their pelagic songs.

And THE BEASTS OF THE SEA call to the swamp dwellers who dream beneath domes of cypress: nimble otters, nesting alligators—

Yet, there are more beautiful encounters still: the cat searching for her person's lover whose Parisian perfume and bodymusk have infused tidy cotton sheets and recycled bedroom air, or you saving the last bite for one you think you may love, or some splendor-struck traveler mailing souvenir postcards back home.

Somewhere in the miracle of space, there is a supernova of fuchsia, white-hot brilliance, citrine, and serpentine all at once.

And SOURCE understands that these encounters with materials of creation are very necessary and lovingly good.

IV

AND IN ANOTHER CHRONICLE OF LOVE, SOURCE sighs, breathes in, and something tender akin to the diaphragm of the universe contracts, flattens, exhales.

And from this space—colored by everything and nothing at all—emerges WONDER perhaps as ectoplasm erupts from your bon vivant great-grandaunt's throat.

In the spaces of dappled light, SOURCE waits as morning light erupts through the caning of Cesca chairs in your lover's breakfast nook.

And THE BEASTS OF THE SEA carry on—wet bodies move in and out of coves, trenches, rock, and sargassum bound only by currents and streams.

Eels as green as peridots formed deep in mantle spawn in mesopelagic twilight and their storied distant kin swim 4,000 miles to live and die and live again.

THEN, the curious magic of cowrie shells unearthed in Ojibwe lands reminds us how the smallest entities move through oceans, sands, and hands held tight from the Maldives to Ghana and Benin, Brazil and Mexico, and beyond between lakes and ice.

Somewhere, an oracle reveals the gathered suspense of ages: a brownskinned GODDESS clothed in ten yards of aquamarine silk, crowned with white roses, and adorned with conch shells, pearls, and seven peacock feathers—she is the mother of all and the very seas of which we enter with awe.

NOW BEAUTY, SONG, AND CHANCE marvel at sugarloaf rubies set in buttery gold and Beluga caviar served in hand-polished nacre. In their field of vision, a chanteuse unravels seven smokey ballads—unnerving lovers already laden with craving and resolve as brittle as hot glass.

DESIRE slithers in, holds the door for IMAGINATION, and for reasons that transcend words, after IMAGINATION, there is a brick. Brick cannot hold and there's no room for sobering thought.

And the brick crumbles.

IMAGINATION gives permission—and sight into future things. And lovers reach toward the scent of violets after rain.

And, for a little while, only WONDER and the inhalation of LOVE remain.

THE IMPRINT

the imprint of my love
	a shell midden around the
coast of a heart
thousands of pieces built up
to shield and guard

you can be vulnerable
	be the apple tree I feed and
I remain
	surrounding the space you
once breathed
	now you are again air

dust water
and I am the middens
of your dreams
	the middens of your ancestors

I am more than the heap
you threw once-fat oysters
into
	I am canal, basin, plaza

TELL ME

Tell me I'm the bivalve mollusk you crave after a day of conversations you had so you can linger a while drinking something minerally, golden white—maybe Italian

Tell me I'm the bivalve mollusk you dress in minced pink, a drop of bright citrus that you position to your lips akin to a kiss and suck down—my tender flesh becomes a part of you

Tell me I'm the bivalve mollusk for which you heat the salted butter—it softens up on your simple counter—not marble but a utilitarian butcher's block marked with love and cuts

Tell me I'm the bivalve mollusk your ancestors farmed in Bretagne—or the one with melon notes from Oléron—and wash me down with chenin blanc and walk back to wherever home is now as light shifts in the city town arrondissement

DREAM

"Oysters are the answer." —M.F.K. FISHER, *Consider the Oyster*

Last night I was oyster
whelmed and moored in sound fed by cool Atlantic expanse
gorged green, deep cupped, plump, and happy.

I remember the time before
when I was spat and sounds of banqueting shrimp lured me. Crackling like
digital fire or hand-cut bacon a lover fries in cast iron the morning after,
fearless and shirtless, humming some jaunty hymn.

I knew I'd be safe—those pistoled shrimp speckled as magpie's eggs
didn't burrow in waiting for me. And I didn't laugh at their cartoonish claw,
something only a god or child would fashion.

But did you know those asymmetric shrimp,
those tiny beacons of delicious possibility,
can shoot a bubble louder than thunder and hot as the surface of the sun?
Well, almost as hot, but—

for a night, I was oyster
my ocean-worn shoulders whelmed and moored in sound fed by
cool Atlantic expanse

and now I am woman who dances in an emerald and schorl silk dress akin to
Carolina green-gill oysters waiting for
full moon.

THERE'S A PLACE WITHOUT OYSTERS

after Pieter Aertsen's A Meat Stall with the Holy Family Giving Alms, *1551*

displacement unsettles
    a refugee crisis
    unrepentant developers
    excess. foreshadowing what?
an end? *the* end?

butchers will butcher
    body land no escape

disgust.

things nameless. unnamable.

no oysters or fat chickens
no hot ovened bread
    a refugee crisis
    unrepentant despots
    excess. foreshadowing death.

the sea has swallowed the shore

hungry. relentless. unrepentant.

no oysters or fat shells
no hot yolky sun but charred spent flesh

always a refugee crisis
always unrepentant escapes

always empty pantries
and now

there's a place without oysters.

THERE CAME TO BE A PLACE WITH NO OYSTERS

In the place with no oysters, there are ancient middens.
They stack three stories: porcelain, sun-bleached, sharp as the blade of your best knife—the one you swear sings if you coax it the right way.

Three stories of wishbones broken with hopes, shells like your great grandmother's foot all bones and arthritis, cracked bowls, shards of vessels that held prayers.

In the place with no oysters, there are stories of thoughts spun into being
then lost to progress.

The others stack remains three stories:
all white and grey and acid-washed blue.
No sound of seabirds or laughter or pleasure gasps.

In the place with no oysters, the ancient middens are laced with silver hair, faded seaweed, tar-covered strands of silk,

bolts and the nail clippings you sent to your beloved so there'd be something left of you when there came to be a place with no oysters.

NO SPACE FOR YOUR GHOST

for Will Morris

Of course I ordered oysters!
Raw? You frowned lovingly and I reached for your hand,
across from us a friend happy I'd found someone—
you—and I am gorged
with desire.

The oysters slicked down my throat and later I
          collapsed
not into your arms because you were busy—had things to do—
but into tears.

So what! It was complicated!
Always was. But now the thought of the hand I held onto knobby veiny forever gone
in a place I can never return
is—

Now development weighs assets.
Value collapses beauty.
Resilience fails and I'm left with an edge of meaning—
          tongue caught grasping toward memory and briny tender flesh.

No room ghostly empty.
No space for your ghost.
Only a no-space I
once ate
          oysters.

OYSTER DREAMS

after Jan Jansz. den Uyl's Banquet Piece, c.1635
for Edward

You burned me down
rendered me like fat
drew out my sacred essence
stole centuries of melancholy

My somber existence obliterated with
your touch—
me holding onto the oyster
sucking its essence

Our first night
silver of your hair like something precious—
I find a strand when I'm hundreds
of miles away

Holding onto my oyster dreams
nowhere to be
released from weighty history I gather my dreams
sup at your banquet

BAD OYSTER

"And live to tell it." —M.F.K. FISHER, *Consider the Oyster*

The stench of shit and suddenly you're in the 19th arrondissement penthouse sandwiched between dancing lights—orbs of splendor diffused with tears—and the wall of his palm.

BLACK BLOOD
WAS IT SHARP MUSTARD?
GRAINS GLASS BLOOD BLACK CAVIAR
WALT WHITMAN

Her dancing lights
Eiffel Tower
searchlight you fear could
illuminate your naked, abandoned flank one day.

WALT WHITMAN
CAVIAR BLACK BLOOD GLASS GRAINS
MUSTARD? SHARP IT WAS
BLOOD BLACK

Suddenly the stench of shit and
the bad oyster beautiful and unassuming until
you gulp it down second-guessing the dog shit that
must be sandwiched between your foot and bar rail.

And you wait—
hope you can keep it
          down
until morning.

II

I ate that oyster.
Inhaled decay as it flittered in
my mouth. Still,
I swallowed.

Fraction of space. Rupture.
Collapse. Intrusion. Don't want to *cry them shame*.
Only a *crisis of truth*. Peculiar nightmare jimmies a lock. Invades.

Me—frozen as Idit—cursed wife—but I don't look back.
I stand. Become pillar. Brace for impact.
Tongue searches for fissures across void. I am nowhere. I am everywhere. Taste
ferrous, salted saliva.

I ate that oyster.
That bad one I couldn't believe because because I must have stepped in something
like that afternoon in Paris—

but no! Decay transports me to penthouse teeming with anthropology artefacts
cries laughter rage
Walt Whitman and Baudelaire
and it is nighttime in the city and the glitter has quit.

I ate that oyster because
I've eaten shit
   and kept it down
'til morning.

III

Yes, you ate that oyster and felt the rush—
that feeling you may have invited the end—
the end in vomit and
shit and groans.

Not the fabulous end you'd prefer, but the one that waited for you in that Parisian penthouse. Probably Black Orchid perfume, plundered artefacts, strands from another woman competing with your own.

The chaos and heartbreaking reality of it all.
Not because you loved him.
YOU PLAYED A ROLE
TO SURVIVE.

But our hearts broke for all that beauty. Shards of glass mixed up with blood and guts and feces. The heartbreaking truth that so many of your memories of beauty—seeing Italy from Fréjus, floating in

The Mediterranean, seeing the dancing lights of the Eiffel Tower for the first time—would be laced with pain, terror, confusion—the NO NO STOP NO, the just-in-case diary for your loved ones,

the "je suis désolée" from the gas station attendant.
THE ADRENALINE OF SURVIVAL.
And you are in awe and shaking as you remember in the bed of another lover.

That bad oyster didn't belong
any more than you did.
And yet you kept it all down—
got out in the morning.

IV

Seven years later and there's no fear, but there's memory memory
tactile slick gummy beyond expiration a foul place now just a midden of memory
but back then a place where he tells lies and I believe him

wait for him to pass out gather my things I shake worry I can't be too quiet but I
make it to the elevator and why I press so many buttons I don't know but it's the
only thing that makes sense

Seven years later and there's only the fear of sepsis, a slow painful gastronomical
death and I imagine my body at home in a bone-colored midden, a record of
12,000 years of love and death and hunger and desire

Filtering memory through my gills I feel the stuck pieces as they wash over me
cloudy mud-colored water and fishy poison, but I know better than to let it
all in now

Seven years ago and now I can hardly believe I've let that bad oyster go down,
threatening collapse failure bile and putrid putrefying things but I get out—
wake up in the morning.

THE BOUNTY OF OCCASION

for the Blancos, Freibergers, and Palshas

Table set with anticipation for shared reflection, Prosecco, and the ruby-colored
vintage saved for this very occasion of full-throated laughter and annual
embraces—this is family: found, chosen, and born into

The fervent negotiation for who will slice, shuck, or shovel—
The swell of Patti LaBelle, Miles Davis, Frank Sinatra, Chet Baker or Nat King
Cole, guitar riffs, and "Stairway to Heaven"—we find ways to come together tracing
fingers over ribbons and butcher's twine unraveling opinions and spaces beneath
the weight of conversation

The sweet, home-like scent of bourbon pecan pie and arguments about "pee-can"
and "puh-kahn" and the aunts who wear diamonds on every finger and patent
leather stilettos

And sometimes there's a place for the ancestor, a sacred setting rimmed in gold or
red, and we open our hearts to the miracle of love, we savor embraces and smiles
we encounter once a year

We launder linens, dust off the crystal, oil our butcher blocks, and then we wait
to toast new loves, old loves, renewed loves, and the bounty of occasion: roasted
oysters harvested the day before, golden she-crab soup, and impossible rum cakes,
and elaborate tiramisu

Rosemary bundles and needles everywhere—the dog barking at flocking swallows
falls silent with the offer of an abnormally large bone

Bliss, joy, and hope fill the room thick—it's a kind of invited breathlessness that
settles into deep-belly rubs, fought yawns, and lower-back caresses

and this is love—deeply rendered and felt like fat cradling tender parts
and this is love—found, chosen, birthed and held, fed and called upon

THE SHAPE OF LOVE

"I have been loved . . . by something strange, and it has forgotten me."
—DJUNA BARNES, *Nightwood*

Now I reach for the shape of love in the absence of light and you are obsidian, India ink, charcoal

I am raw stretched canvas, cold-pressed toothy paper, unbleached cotton

Now I reach for the shape of love in the absence of light and you are black sesame, tamari, Kaluga caviar

I am perfumed rice, undressed mackerel, the finest oyster you gingerly pried open

Now I reach for the shape of love in the absence of light and you are ether, vapor, forgotten pheromones

I am morning glory, night blooming cereus, tender wandering moonflower

Now that I have grasped the shape of love in the absence of light
all the colors have gone—no powdery rose, fragrant lilac, hypnotic hyacinth
I drink and feel nothing
I can't not remember what I wanted to love about you

I remember but I cannot continue

You a void I wanted to fill and feel—

Now I fear your gaze, your voice, your touch
The colors have gone and I don't want them to return

I refuse the intoxicating lily, your sleight of hand

You, well-positioned oyster knife

Me, hiding beneath my spiny shell

You—all blade, yet I want the cut, still, the fissure of membrane

You, shiny body I wanted to love with invitation
but no welcome remains

Now I reach for the shape of love in the absence of light and you are obsidian, India ink, charcoal

I am raw stretched canvas, cold-pressed toothy paper, unbleached cotton

NACRE

Grit enters and I am hot, agitated, madder
red   left wanting
                wanting to be whole once more but this thing
                this small rough irregular thing has come inside

like the look you give me for a moment in the morning
subdued by piggy bank pink, egret cotton, and our mingled skins indented
        resistant as memory foam

I want your gritty love
                from an ocean of detritus—organic and plastic and unknown
                turquoise blanket, fluid seaweed, nylon fishing nets
still—even if it makes me ill because

nacre.   Movement filtering fashions pearl
inside of me born with luminescent wallpapered hull
        and I am no mother and

I let you come inside
I let you in—opened just wide enough for you to leave me
harboring
                harboring something unexpected
precious with glints of mauve, silver, and mica

and I have entered you
you: thorny oyster tell me

tell me you want my grit—
                from ocean unfathomed deep indigo, silk and saline

tell me I haven't come in vain
tell me I've made you hot, angry, agitated and left you wanting
                    wanting to be whole once more but

Your silence hollows me
still—and now

I have become siren, a hallowed hollow singing thing—
fashioned smooth as marble, sharp as obsidian, and tough as flint
                    by the blades of nearly 100 men

And this thing you left inside lingers wrapped in nacre:
mother of pearl

MY HEART'S LEFT FOOT

your breath is salt in wound of memory
and I lust to forget your wily razor cuts
my heart rendered into oyster
gilled and shellkept

our first kiss on my golden couch, sweet—
now I labor to disrelish your mustached crooked smile,
your curious eyes bagged with jetlag and debauch
you say you "value our time" but

my heart's left foot anchors
as oyster to hard clean things,
and wants to meet you again—
but we both know you won't allow yourself a clean slate

—me wearing rabbit *ushanka*, January fire, and you
less aloof yet bitter enough for me to know better
now I'm left dressing your memory
my whole being becomes wound

I don't want to write more poems about you
I force myself shut, beg cilia, "let me starve!"
because I am full of your water, the stuff you've
left behind

I have relished you too long
harvest me, dredge me—rake me from desire
now I have become a bitter thing
brilliant amaro, something rued

I want to be radiant in your dreams
I want you to labor ways to reintroduce yourself to me
I want my breath to be longing in
your innermost chambers beet red and verdigris

I wish you thought about me coming
to leave you gifts in the borrowed mailbox you rarely checked,
and me shaking in morning light in that suckling pig-pink room,
stroking some apotropaic thing

because even then I feared it'd be the last morning we'd share
then you made French press in the borrowed kitchen
belonging to an heiress and I inherit
you, the sharp-footed whelk at once golden, magnificent,

tightly coiled ready to bore into my oystered heart,
my whole oystered self
wounded, digested
shellchipped and breathless

I FEEL SAFE WITH YOU

You smell clean and

I fell into your skin
couldn't get it off
moved into it as if I were lucky oyster crab

your buttersoft, justwarm skin—color of nacre in moonlight—
nestled between mine and bed.

I feel safe with you.
As I dream
deepsleep snores filter through

and the dirty mophaired dog is sleeping by the front door.

You feel like someone I could love
and you said it was okay for me to be vulnerable.
Of course, I have to wonder, but I wished—then

with you, I sailed into a new year
as the waning gibbous moon moved from
Libra into Scorpio.

And in my own bed, between linen and silk, my lips reach for your skin
wish you'd call for me in the night.

BLUE NEVUS

for Francis Ponge

blue nevus, black pearl
you take your place above my deep brown eye
        beneath curled lashes, my black lace

you, blue nevus, fascinate me. I see dark nebulae,
but when I ask, the doctor says you're just a mole

yet, scientists see the kinship
black pearls from black-lipped oysters
        and we know a pearl forms   *sous un firmament de nacre*
        beneath a sky that is also its mother

and I learn that three percent of the global population is impacted
        affected   marked   *sous un firmament du ciel*
        beneath sky held by arch of sky

240 million or thereabouts see blue nevus reflected
a whole universe beneath each mole

this blueblack thing on my forehead—
        I remember the beauty mark I prayed for as a browncolored teen not
        considering the strangeness of how some marks are beautiful and others must
        be concealed

a forehead one lover once loved
a beautymarked forehead I hold high
        beneath a sky that is also my mother

THIS IS THE WAY

this is the way I fall in love
with an ocean of salt and bleached coral
I dream of ways to repair doctor nurse restore rescue renew this
        reef
reaching for branches and recording the comings and goings of fish wet and scaled
and plucky as zither and
I fall

        so easily
        your poison dart has already speared my naked heel and
who are you to judge
me?
        So what?   I fall in love with drowning men in deserted places
I fall in love

I said I fall in love

OUVRIR

up up up so many stairs spiraling sweat
thick cobwebs tucked neatly in corners then up up up more a loft with some man's records vinyl in July heat through frosted glass

then up up up a tight steep spiral another loft within a loft white wooden and soft
beneath two skylights

on Boulevard de Charonne at the edge of the eleventh arrondissement, I had a dream and there was the magic word, and I woke up repeating it over and over and
over

ouvrir ouvrir ouvrir ouvrir ouvrir

I speak the best French in my dreams
ouvrir ouvrir ouvrir ouvrir ouvrir

to open to begin to initiate to turn on to switch on to put on to open onto to lead into to open up to be open to to confide in to make to create to cut something open to gash something

gash me open cut me membrane muscle bruise me on some stranger's stoop and I will open again
again and

je te chercherai comme une petite souris cherchant du fromage

I lied I don't want to stop with you I am open initiated led into something risky and then *couvrir* cover me cover cover *couvrir* confide in me abide in me just for the time it takes us to eat a dozen oysters and then a dozen more and more—

always the oysters leading us back into opening up and it is just sex and it's also something else but that something else *une autre chose* doesn't have to ruin everything else and—

ouvrir ouvrir ouvrir ouvrir ouvrir

a few nights before I dreamed of the magic word, I dreamed of you through the
cover of space and something else unnamable
and then we traveled along a canyon together

there are things I did not tell you because I am afraid you wouldn't believe
but what you call fun is the most passion I've felt in years and like any drug, your
eyes your mouth your hair your hand in mine are things I cannot forget

ouvrir ouvrir ouvrir ouvrir ouvrir

open open open open open me like an oyster from a roadside stand in some northeastern place shaped by family business

I am always that dreaming woman up up up a tight spiral stair on Boulevard de Charonne

I am always that woman who lives at the end of the gravel road with the wild yard of mugwort winter jasmine hyacinth mimosa salvia that surrounds house and bed I often leave unmade where I have dreamed of you with no vestige of possession—you are not my own and you are free

and for whatever time we have or had, je suis

ouvrir ouvrir ouvrir ouvrir ouvrir

ANOTHER TIME

for Rosa Guy

In another time, I'd be your mistress—*demi-mondaine* if we both were lucky
    but in this one, you haunt my dreams
    (*mais pour quelques instants, nous nous amusions*)

At 4 a.m., your face, a selenic thing, hovers
I feel your breath as I grasp the edges of dream
    searching for my hands to keep me cemented in dream as oyster to oyster
    in reef

Within seconds your face becomes another then another then—
    me, startled, my mouth marble full—
    yet somehow I

call you back.
Your face again luminous as moon full
    (*reviens vers moi*)

At 4:07, I wake myself with the thunder of your name on my tongue
    two syllables I've found myself saying in secret under
    covers

Have I no shame? "Another time" is what I want! Am I alone in this desire?
Will you remember me, brief lover I may be?
    (*autre fois autre fois je veux une autre fois*)   yet the ghosts of Delphi

murmur still
as muse surveilling her lover on his wedding day
    —the unnerving presence of sex and sin

So in another time, I'd be your love and we'd both be lucky
    and we'd eat green-gilled oysters under Jupiter on Rue de Charonne and
    drink gorgeous chenin blanc

I want your wine-fed kiss, the squeeze of your hand as we cross through the night
Ask me what I'm thinking and I won't say only half of it
    this time

500 METERS

you could flirt a little—

speak French like a fifth grader ramble on about the American music
"vous aimez musique américaine?"
and he hears "vous avez...?" while he's trying to remember what the
middle-aged couple ordered and he's already forgotten your beaujolais or
was it something white?
"non, vous aimez..." you repeat
and there's the mental note about how the tuna is warmer and less salted
than you expected and you're too polite to ask for salt—it's the most
gourmand restaurant in the square after all, and you walked an hour a mess
of sweat and desire and a story too but the jasmine rice et champignons are
memorable and you say "oui, tout est parfait!"

even make a fool you'll never see him again but you don't make a fool and decline
the headlamp he offered and a potential morning rendezvous not a rendezvous, a
drop off, a passage through a doorway, and you walk—

sun setting streetlights becoming more scarce
only 500 meters of darkness he said
500 meters
headlights whizz by you retreat to margin, grass no-shoulder-of-road maybe
stars but you're wearing new clogs and your feet are tired and then

crossroads 8-minute-walk until home-for-now-home or forest way or D137

(and that you only know later and you think about how 37 is one of your
favorite numbers—why you can't say)

but the 8-minute walk is a blanket of ink: you're enveloped by darkness so dark
you feel something primal fear of the void and an intuition that says no, no stop
walking, don't—

yes, you should've called the Uber at the restaurant but you thought "12 euros is a lot for 8 minutes" and now you're waiting 9, 11, 15 and hoping the driver stops (and you only know later that his name is Foly and he chastises you for booking the ride "C'est dangereux!" he says and maybe asks if you're crazy: "Êtes-vous fou?")

and you hear the spiders making webs—
wait for things to crawl up your legs.

SALMON WALKS INTO A BAR

after Matthew Broussard

for Terrance Hayes and Night School Bar

Salmon walks into a bar.
Let's not worry about how—it happened and
he sat on a worn-green leather stool—
the kind with the chrome base, but that's not important

Bartender says *hello, what can I do ya for?* and
Salmon says, *oh whatever you think is good* and
before Salmon can take in the view of glass and liquid—brown and
clear and gold with labels of paper and foil

Bartender says *let me hook you up*
(and no, that's not the joke)
and he makes Salmon a gin martini—shaken not stirred and
Salmon is pleased with the process

Thank you, Salmon says to the bartender who's
thinking of sinister things

You know, we have a color named for you
Bartender says to Salmon with knife-edge eye
and Salmon is sipping cautiously as there's no one to
skål!

Oh really? asks Salmon
Is it a beautiful silvery glinty hue?
No says Bartender
It's pink.

I WILL NOT LOOK AWAY

for Julia Kristeva

"Sometimes one meets a woman who is beast turning human. . . . Such a woman is the infected carrier of the past: before her the structure of our head and jaws ache—we feel that we could eat her, she who is eaten death returning, for only then do we put our face close to the blood on the lips of our forefathers." —DJUNA BARNES, *Nightwood*

I am in a season of nascent love with only cries and gestures—
Unfat and Hungered.

I grow plump with nectar—my milkteeth fall out and crumble into unvarnished fossils of whom I mused to become. Canines incisors molars and more—
I encounter the Real.

Feed me, I cry.

And then you scurry onto shore. *Feed me.*
Roaring surf caresses you with dappling light and I dredge your soft-shelled body with my gaze.

I will not look away. I am some newfangled Gorgon but my mothers taught me well and I will fry you whole. Eat you legs eyes mouth and all.

And now I am surf, brilliant and blue and you cannot escape even if you were to return—

This is a spell to wrap your silver-set onyx up in my pink raw tourmaline and rutilated quartz. I sing.

You be dredged, fried, and eaten: now a part of my Breath, my Blood, my Bones, my Chansons, and the traces I will leave behind.

I am ocean, I am Chora, hungry for your meat.

3: EKPHRASTIC ENCOUNTERS

When I did slither,
you saw me coming hungry
opened up so wide, I leapt.

A TANGLE OF DESIRE

after Gerhard Richter's Station (577-2), *1985*
for Gordon

with you
I feel shy, like a second grader with
my New Kids On The Block lunchbox

burning lust that I can't name
but I want you to see my
Lisa Frank notebook

you bring up colors in me
I am vermillion
you, Aegean blue

I'm too young to know or name
the colors, but you
see me, look past my lunchbox
and
invite me to sit by you

we ride the bus

now woman I am seeing you
seeing me
hot pink, chartreuse
soft hunter

HIBERNAL VOYAGE

after David Bowie's "Fantastic Voyage" (1979)
for Gordon

my soft belly, your drunken heart
take us places where all our knit-together
fears dissolve

our mirth cracks clay, echoes into the
inky expanse, peppers it white with wishes

we unearth passageways, caverns
lined with mink, cashmere
cool, ferrous earth

wrapped in animal heat
we surface, wander through

lipstick red camellias, saffron yellow jasmine
render us rapt, held by
fragrant edges of winter

PINK DRIPS CALLED MAUVE

after Georges Le Chevallier's Baked Goat Cheese with Garden Lettuces (after Chef Alice Waters), 2015

We made love beneath the
Pollack, raw with man angles and
abstract expression

we deconstructed a language
through our sex we birthed
rust, sharp fir tree needles, messy
unboundness

    we coupled toward Frankenthaler
pink drips called mauve as
we consumed spiritual chaos
round with messy shapes, subtle
beauty *you* called shibui

There, Pollack unbothered by
our shapes of verdant green,
red blood

1960S, DEEP LILAC

after George Bireline's Matisse Window, *1964*
for Edward

New Orleans held your magic before
I was born and when I think about the 1960s—that
ecstasy-birthed generation
I clamor for your windowsill
your bedroom, deep lilac in low light
on the avenue named for the saint of bachelors and dogs
and I remember you pinked with pleasure
the pool of your dog's jealous piss and me
naked in your kitchen chair now morning lit and still
as the gilded Maid of Orleans watches from a mile away.
Later, a splinter in my finger reminds me I'm alive.

CLAY LUNGS OBSCURE INTIMACY

after Helen Frankenthaler's Captain's Watch, *1986, and Robert Motherwell's* Two Figures, *1960*

My muted echo of a voice
is like putty
                    sticky with risk and gestures
of captivity.

It figures your clay lungs would
make no room for intimacy.
                    No room for a voyage beyond
that home bruised scar.

Chocolate melts in your gaze
but not me. I am slate. Waiting
          and there's no pleasure, no river
no blood.

Clay lungs obscure intimacy
sing only muddy mesas, sticky like putty.

NEW MEXICO IN MY DREAMS

after Richard Diebenkorn's Berkeley No. 8, *1954*

Cornflower blue running through rock,
fractured crags

The somethingcolored puff of
roadrunner

I don't find myself longing for the Southwest
          but

movement, synthesis, and no plan
take me there

And I'm parched from white lies
slick crimson stopped up trying

trying try—
remember why I left

MENSTRUATION

after Adolph Gottlieb's Phoenix Burst, *1973*

Crush crash drip smear I sop up
broken matter debris detritus
deathly red and silky

I am made from soil and atomic
matter and dust from asteroids
I am a dancing kinetic collage of
wounds and wounding

Falling more into love with my being
like Krasner after Pollack
menstruation compresses burns
brings metal clanging around I drink
tea, burst into tears splattering
down like coal, tar

I remember tripping up falling—
smelling the blood careening from
my empty womb
thick like resin tacky clotted
and free

The first blood bright red on
white cotton like the flag over
Japan
          bright—hopeful phoenix rising

SHADOWS OF HER THORNED DRESS

after Alison Saar's Tippy Toes, *2007*

Clothes that don't fit are captivity
She remembers the crinoline, aubergine
très cher—
                                        but what does *she* want?

She feels confined in her own skin—
no ownership of her body
but that relentless *come nigh,* the beckoning of
barbed wire hoop skirts

She with outstretched arms and raw
rough-hewn tippy toes—
                                        her ascension was *slick—*
metallic like the tooled perfection of Rodin

But clothes that don't fit are captivity
and the crinoline is torn
the bodice all thorned with lace—
                                        that lies

Now her shadows cry beauty and open betrayal
wooden arms reaching for
ultramarine, indigo memory
that *come nigh—*
                                        fragile as twigs

A DOMESTIC WORKER'S PRAYER

after Minnie Evans's The Tree of Life, *1962*

for my mom

Fuchsia-filled azaleas and emerald leaves
I thought I'd left the garden
I thought Eden died with that tree.
What gatekeeper keeps rules and
order here in this place lush, ancient, and hot
enough to melt the wax that fills
your white-tailed visionary dreams?

PIECES OF GRANDMOTHER

after Sam Gilliam's Sawtooth, *1980*
for my grandmother, Georgie

Grandmother. I wish I had a sort of
yolk-colored devotion to you. One that
dances and prays before an altar
for the Day of the Dead.

One that transports me back to
sunset at Holden Beach when I
held tenuously to a love I imagined
you would've loved.

Buttery daylilies and climbing roses. Chain link
fences, white stucco, mealy pears
and rumors of dog food, nascent dementia
and

cake batter, seeing van Gogh's sunflowers in Paris.
Yearning for timeworn connections
fibers transmissions that move like
blood, brain matter.

Rubies set in 14 karat gold, powdery blush
mauve and jazz records race
records bricks thrown for civil
rights at buses held together by irregular pieces of metal
hybrid, gutted as

the tooth I placed beneath my pillow.
Grandmother, the mark you've left
on me like a collaged canvas
seeking a deft hand—

WATER GODDESS

after an Anang Ibibio artist's Mami Wata Figure *from mid-20th C*

You offend with your precarious beauty:
wreck havoc, steal riches, testify to the passing of whole generations.
You charmer! You snake in the grass!
Your beauty is your hybridity—your
ability to curse and love in one
breath!

I, a mirror to no one. Yet, a reprint
of my parents.
My parents who use paper calendars with Indian goddesses that could be
Nigerian or German
        or is it the other way around?

But you—every fiber of you slithers
like snakecharmers in the square:
"If you look, you take picture, you pay!"
they say.

But you
        rust and shards of glass some mistake
for rubies and diamonds
        transformed and transfixed by your
peculiar beauty your wealth   you—an
icon in the dreams of mothers and
their children—

and I. Me. Still a mirror to no one.
Reprinted and unrepentant.

I DO NOT SWIM NOR DO I HAVE MANICURED GRASS

after Matthew Brandt's Long Lake, WA 10, *2012*
for my dad

Mourning swimming. I used to float
dive go under and emerge
submerge myself with my best friend
in chemically blue water.

Now there's loss. Another piece of
shame. Something my dad would
not be proud to know:
his firstborn can no longer swim.

My memory of swimming like a damaged
film made too hot by a sun raging as
the fires of Mordor
    curling edges like the hair I tried to

protect from reversion.
    Black girls know.
That was an easy excuse to stay out of
the water—me craving soft ripples,

warm weather, the smell of freshly
manicured grass.   But swimming is a relic
like a postcard I send to another's husband
boyfriend ex-husband

—here I am! In solitude in some foreign
place. Maybe there's a mountain, fir,

aspen, hard-to-follow directions, and then
the best merguez and fries I've ever had.

But mourning swimming—a lost love. Because I
loved submerging my body and moving through
a wash,
          a streak of warm brown in azure.

CODA

I do not weep at the world—I am too busy sharpening my oyster knife.

—**ZORA NEALE HURSTON,**
How It Feels to Be Colored Me

MY FINAL FORM

So is this *this?* my final form?
Burrowed into seabed, rested, resting wet sand, fragments of shell, rock, decay
particles wash over under in through
Somewhere there is giant swirling gyre gorged with
invasive particles in endless blue and green
plastic spans micro meso macro mega
is there beauty in this terribly sublime arrangement of detritus, cast-off human things?
This toxic skein a sort of skinsuit shed at dawn at dusk at every minute of every single
day debris slips in filters
through heart, kidney,
muscle, and
now I me—a curving curvy thing ridges graceful dip crest dip crest dip

dancing tentacles masquerading as pocketbook of teeth

Am I oyster?
Beanblack mussel?
Strong-footed clam?

I remember too much
Memory encumbered with presence and my nose, a finely-tuned machine
something I've stretched and prodded in mirrors lamenting size
remembering clothespins and the blemishes hidden beneath brown skin
the eventual drooping of time but not yet
the cotton consumed by witch hazel alpha lipoic acid retinol and tansy

and the mimosa layered between French perfume and tears—salted with memories of
lovers gone into the night and
what is a life? What is a lifespan
other than a thistle, a corn-yellow sunflower with coffeeground head
a perfect cabochon of jade
and the detritus that comes at the end? Aubergine
bruises bloom and we wait for the next place:
emerald palace, pristine marble floors
a hall of mirrors gilt in gold—a veritable Versailles and sunlight

Sunlight feels like falling in love and I'm left with presence the swell of
radiance in the afternoon on my brownskin skin

And I remember my grandmother's persimmon tree
fire-lapping orange, collapsing into tangerine cream then cherry red
chiggers and bites and heat and the metallic bubbling of chainsaw teeth

And I can do more than just sense the danger ghost nets ghost men
toxic and alluring
and the diver who'll cut out my muscle and waste the rest
the hungry, multi-armed starfish
or the sneaking ray
and I have to wonder. Did the ancients look at me—see me, see me? Did they
see my blue eyes and understand? Did they know that I could see?

I see. I see. I know danger because I sense *and* see?

And did they model the buda, kitab, mati, the apotropaic thing with myriad names—
after me?

My eyes—

eyes eyes eyes

200 bottlecap blue nazars brilliant as Sri Lankan sapphires

200 telescopes made of fishglint and whatever transforms chameleon into some magical hidden thing—

And I swim.

Propel myself with miniature jet stream.
Me, powered by something no smaller than the dry U-10 you slather in warm butter.

But I swim.

Clacking comically like the wind-up teeth that chased you awake after a feverish night
or the dentures you saw your grandmother remove for the first time:
CLACK CHOMP CLACK *I'm comin to gitcha* she says with mischief- and love-laced smile.

AND I SWIM.
And I am free, unmoored. No anchor.

I am no oyster.
I am no beanblack mussel.
Not even a strong-footed clam.

Me. Now I am become sea scallop
a curving curvy thing with ridges dipping gracefully cresting up and resting down with dancing tentacles, a Venusian purse of hirsute teeth.

NOTES

So much of this book is tied to place. And time. And memory.

"Black, holy time" comprises the preface and is ekphrastic in spirit, but isn't ekphrastic like the other poems in this collection. It began with the line "I'm an ecstatic pedestrian who moves with grace" I wrote in "Passing Their Word: An Oral History/Playwriting Workshop" led by Slyvester Allen, Jr. The workshop was a part of the 2024 The Commons: Southern Futures at the University of North Carolina (UNC)-Chapel Hill's Carolina Performing Arts lineup. This poem's first line references an earlier unpublished ekphrastic poem I wrote for Lina Iris Viktor's site-specific installation *Triumvirate: Constellations I, IV, IX,* at the North Carolina Museum of Art (NCMA) (2016, 2017/8, 2020).

Altarworks are poems for people who've passed on—some I've known and love. I imagine the poems being a part of an altar thick with candles and melted wax like my own.

In "Valentine's day," Defeat is the name of the Five of Swords in the Thoth Tarot.

"Mimosan" is named for the Mimosa tree (*Albizia julibrissin*), and in herbal medicine, Mimosa is used for heartache and grieving.

"One side of the border" is a poem about losing loved ones to suicide—but from the decedent's perspective. I thank Jaki Shelton Green for asking me what would happen if I removed the word "suicide" from the poem. More than a year later, I did that and made a few small revisions. And then I thought about Toni Morrison's decision to use "love" sparingly in *Love* (2003) and how in doing so, she explains, "it could become an earned word" and continues: "If I could give the word, in my very modest way, its girth and its meaning and its terrible price and its clarity at the moment when that is all there is time for, then the title does work for me" (quoted in Houston 2).

In "See me now," the rooftop is at Jnane Tamsna, Morocco's first Black-owned hotel, founded by Meryanne Loum-Martin and her husband Gary Martin. Defeat is the name of the Five of Swords in the Thoth Tarot. The poem also references flower, gem, and mineral essences made by friend, poet, herbalist, artist, and musician Chanelle Allesandre for Moon by Moon Apothecary. I ate the meal featuring Fine de Claires №3 at Clamato in Paris, France. The line "Returned to and left and returned again to my perch drenched in Yves Klein blue where I have dreamed and poemed. I bathed in the coral wet room, soaked and caught breath" is an homage to the Visionary suite at Dreamers by Dreamers Welcome in Wilmington, NC. I researched and wrote many poems in that magical third-floor suite.

Henri Matisse's *Les Bêtes De La Mer* (1950) inspires not only the eponymous poem but resonates throughout the entire second part. In what feels like kismet, in high school, I completed a master copy of Matisse's work when I thought I'd become a professional visual artist one day. Twenty years later, at my solo writing residency in The Library of Le Trait d'Union in Samois-sur-Seine, France, I opened John Elderfield's *Henri Matisse: a Retrospective* (1992) and found my way to *Les Bêtes De La Mer* and began thinking about all the marine life that had already become a part of my manuscript. I accepted the challenge to push the mantle further, as it were, and continue with the theme. Thus, passionate love, heartbreak, cheekiness, and more research into marine life than I ever imagined imbue this part of the book. M.F.K. Fisher's *Consider the Oyster* (1941) recommended by the aforementioned Chanelle (before I set out to finish this book in Wilmington, NC, the first time) is a remarkable food and travel narrative and source of accessible marine biology. The notion that an "oyster leads a dreadful but exciting life" reigns true (Fisher 3).

The shrimp in "Dream" are pistol shrimp or alpheidae. Look them up. They're amazing little beings.

The "Bad oyster" poems are about my vacation to Fréjus and Paris in August 2016—the first time I'd traveled overseas. And that summer in France, I experienced the most traumatic events of my life. Three months prior, I'd completed my Ph.D. and submitted my dissertation, "Haunted Narratives: The Afterlife of Gothic Aesthetics in Contemporary Transatlantic Women's Fiction." And in a surreal turn of events, I found myself in some of the most beautiful places in the world only to ironically become something of a Gothic heroine myself. To sum it up, the man I went to see wasn't the person he was when I'd met him 18 months before. He was unstable, violent, and cruel. Seven years later, it's summer 2023, and I'm eating oysters in an upscale restaurant, and I don't realize a less-than-lovely oyster until it's too late. It's strange how something so beautiful can be rotten. And suddenly, memories from my first time in France came rushing back. For seven years, I struggled to write about what happened to me, although I'd occasionally return to read the travel diary I kept. The bad oyster was a catalyst. I give endless thanks to the woman, now a dear friend, who answered the U.S. Embassy's emergency line. She was covering another person's shift that Saturday. She generously invited me into her home, and after some coaxing, I said "yes" and spent the rest of my vacation with her and several women in a gorgeous flat in the 16th arrondissement of Paris. Without her kindness which opened the door to healing and joy, I might not have wanted to return to France.

In "Bad oyster II," with "crisis of truth," I reference Cathy Caruth's *Unclaimed Experience* (1996)—a text I reread many times in graduate school, a text that helped me understand my own trauma.

After visiting my dermatologist about the mole on my forehead, I learned it is a benign blue nevus. Its presence brought to mind nacre and how pearls form and I knew I had to write "Blue nevus." I wondered if someone else had recognized and written about the similarity. And, wow, someone had. Thanks to Jefferson Alfredo de Barros et al for their article, "Comparative dermatology: Blue nevus" in *Anais Brasileiros de Dermatologia* (August 2012). This poem also references a line from Francis Ponge's poem "L'huître" ("The oyster") in his collection *Le Parti Pris des Choses* (1942): "*sous un firmament (à proprement parler) de nacre*" which translates to "under a firmament (properly speaking) of mother of pearl."

Ekphrastic poems comprise the book's third section. The one exception is "Hibernal voyage," which contains lines from an unpublished poem I wrote in the style of David Bowie's "Fantastic Voyage" (1979). Many of the artworks referenced are part of the NCMA's permanent collection. I encourage readers to research the artwork or visit in person if they happen to be on view at NCMA or elsewhere. Many thanks to museum employees and friends Brye Shepard and Angela Lombardi for giving me the space to create engaging, inclusive ekphrastic poetry workshops. I wrote many of these poems in the workshops while keeping track of the time. Thanks to the students who've participated over the years—some of whom wrote their first poems.

"My final form," the coda, is an ekphrastic poem in spirit. I began taking notes for this poem during Patrizia Ferreira's artist talk for her solo exhibition *Precarious Habitats* in September 2024 at Meredith College in Raleigh, North Carolina. Fragments of unpublished poems I wrote in one of the aforementioned workshops at NCMA are present. Hence, Joan Mitchell's *Sunflower II* (1972) and Richard Pousette-Dart's *Celebration, Birth* (1976) comprise this final poem as well.

A late introduction to Euell Gibbons' *Stalking the Blue-Eyed Scallop* (1964) by friend and marine biologist Marcus Rich (during my final solo writing retreat in Wilmington, NC) convinced me my intuition to write about the magnificent scallop was apropos. After I wrote "my final form," I returned to Gibbons' text and was struck by his observation:

> The scallop's mobility enables it to escape danger, to seek out water that is rich in oxygen and foodstuffs, and to distribute its species widely. No one who has watched scallops flitting about the tide pools and shallows will deny that they have an instinct for play as well as for survival. They seem to express the joy of life also by the colors they wear.

And so it is.

WORKS CITED

Fisher, M.F.K. *Consider the Oyster*. NYC, North Front Press, 1988.

Houston, Pam. "The Truest Eye." *O, The Oprah Magazine* (November 2003).

ACKNOWLEDGMENTS

I thank the following journals and editors for originally publishing these poems:

"Black, holy time" in *The Commons Crit, Southern Futures, Carolina Performing Arts* (June 2025)

"Ancestors" and "I, Origin" in *Honey Literary*'s issue 1 (2021)

"Valentine's Day" in *Thoughts on the Power of Goodness,* edited by Timothy F. Crowley and Jaki Shelton Green (2020)

"Three of Swords" in *Spread the Word: A Pandemic Open Mic Anthology,* edited by Richard Krawiec, Natalie Eleanor Patterson, and friends (2021)

"Mimosan" in *Kaleidoscope Journal* issue 1 (2021)

"Two Wings" in *Southern Cultures* (November 2020)

"Rhythm, Surrender" and "Oyster Dreams" in Foundation bar menus, edited by Chris Tonelli (Raleigh, NC) in Winter 2022 and Winter 2024, respectively

"There's a place without oysters" and "There came to be a place with no oysters" in *Feminist Studies* 50.2 (Winter 2024)

"The Bounty of Occasion" appeared in *WALTER* (November 2024)

"500 Meters" originally appeared in *Casserole Series Journal,* Walk, issue 1 (2024)

"A Tangle of Desire," "Pink Drips Called Mauve," and "Clay Lungs Obscure Intimacy" in *Triangle Poetry Journal* (2022)

Amorak Huey and Han VanderHart, thank you both for saying yes to my manuscript and for loving my poems. I've so enjoyed working with you two.

Thank you to my generous, thoughtful readers Gabrielle Calvocoressi, Jaki Shelton Green, Alexis Pauline Gumbs, and Emilia Phillips. Your spirits and your words are magic.

Thank you to the beautiful poetry communities of Durham and the broader North Carolina Triangle and Triad. Y'all are a great, lively bunch.

I'm deeply grateful to have a wealth of friends near and far who encourage, inspire, and love me. There are too many of you to list here, but I thank you all for your phone calls, hugs, memes, voice notes, and texts back. Thanks for saying yes to dinners, lunches, drinks, coffee, laughs, shopping trips, art adventures, wine tastings, dancing with toddlers, petting dogs, and so much more.

Thanks to the countless people I've met in restaurants, cafes, and bars who've been generous with their time and shared their passions. I've learned so much and have developed a deeper appreciation for the beautiful meals and drinks I've experienced.

Thanks to the mentors, teachers, professors, advisors, family members, and benevolent ancestors who've sustained and encouraged my creative development.

I thank oceans and waterways, loves and lovers—some here, some gone, some brief, some long.

I thank my parents, Brenda and Herbert, for their love and support, and for naming me Jameela. I'm grateful to have read "I do not swim nor do I have manicured grass" to my dad two days before he died.

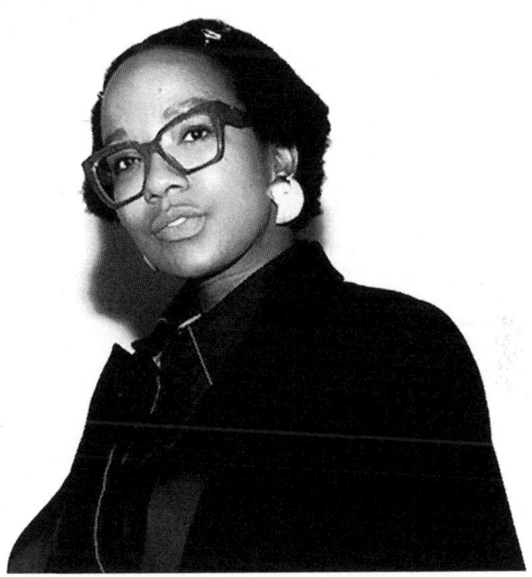

PHOTO: SASSS WORLD

JAMEELA F. DALLIS lives in Durham, NC. Her publications include poems, interviews, arts journalism, and literary scholarship in *Feminist Studies, Honey Literary, The Fight and the Fiddle, Our State, Walter, The Bloomsbury Handbook to Toni Morrison*, and elsewhere. She's inspired by memory and desire, the thrill of wandering new cities, and the wonder of everyday encounters. Her work explores texture, taste, sound, sensation, and the richness of visual art. She curated *Material Encounters* (Peel Gallery, Carrboro, March 2024), juried *Scaffold* (Artspace, Raleigh, April 2023), and has served on regional curatorial and fellowship committees. Jameela has taught dozens of university courses and facilitated creative workshops for more than a decade. Originally from Chattanooga, TN, Jameela received her B.A. in English from the University of New Mexico, Albuquerque, and holds both an M.A. and Ph.D. in English from UNC-Chapel Hill. *Encounters for the Living and the Dead* is her first book of poetry. Read more about her work at jameeladallis.com.

RIVER RIVER BOOKS was founded by Amorak Huey and Han VanderHart in March 2022. Inspired by the idea that you cannot step in the same river twice, two poetry editors join together to publish (at least) two exceptional poetry titles a year, as well as the Plainwater Nonfiction Series.

Poetry Catalog

An Eye in Each Square, Lauren Camp, 2023
Bullet Points: A Lyric, Jennifer A Sutherland, 2023
Dear Memphis, Rachel Edelman, 2024
A Geography That Does Not Hurt Us, Carla Sofia Ferreira, 2024
Pastoral, 1994, Joe Wilkins 2025
Your Mother's Bear Gun, Corrie Williamson, 2025
Field Notes, E.G. Cunningham, 2025
Encounters for the Living and the Dead, Jameela F. Dallis, 2025
Antibody, Elane Kim, 2026
House of Myth and Necessity, Jennifer A Sutherland, 2026
Scythe, Elizabeth Sylvia, 2026
Fifty Mothers, Preeti Vangani, 2026
The Visible Field, Zoë Ryder White, 2026

Plainwater Nonfiction Series

There Is News Along the Ohio River, Beth Gilstrap, 2026
Backyard Alchemy, J.D. Ho, 2026